The Mind Configurator

Author and tool creator:

Totukani Amen II

First Edition

ISBN   978-1-949432-99-2

Published by:

Inner Alchemy's Publishing Inc.
332 S. Michigan Ave.
Ste 1032-C141
Chicago, IL 60604-4434

info@inneralchemys.com
www.inneralchemys.com

Printed in the United States of America

Disclaimer

Tool Progress

Introduction

Thank you for your purchase of 'The Mind Configurator' which was first brought to the public in the year 2012. The Mind Configurator was developed as a tool for deeper introspective exploration of one's mind for personal improvement as well as a tool for professional use.

How did The Mind Configurator come about initially?

It was brought about via deep transcendental states of meditation where the mechanisms of the mind, its mental, emotional, and intellectual connections can be observed and experienced in its totality. This is experienced in such a way where direct change can be injected within one's own internal mind-scape or utilized as a tool within professional environments to help another.

How to use The Mind Configurator?

The focus of this book is introducing the reader to a simple but powerful tool which can be used to help; but if used incorrectly could potentially harm. We will be focusing on the emotional mind to balance and potentially reverse negative thoughts and behaviors. The other uses of The Mind Configurator overall will not be focused on but they do indeed exist. Some of these techniques are so powerful that it would be irresponsible and quite foolish for me to put in writing due to its propensity to bring harm.

If you would like to partake in deeper analysis via The Mind Configurator join the mailing list where any events would be announced.

To join mailing list please visit: www.mindconfigurator.com

The Mind Configurator has been so effective over the years that many practitioners experience profound change in their mental states via the creation of their first configurator. Configurator's can go more than a dozen levels deep which you will learn about later but change has been experienced at only 2-3 levels.

The last event where beginner discussion of the methods found in this book took place was on June 9th, 2018. At these events participants are able to ask as many questions which were needed to begin their own configurator for deeper self-discovery.

One of the most important reasons for discovery, development and subsequent release of this tool was to help humanity move forward. It seems that in certain fields of mental health those who're suffering aren't actually receiving the help that they are crying out for. They're tired of asking why. What are some of the why's that those who suffer typically ask to no avail?

1. Why do I think the way that I do?

2. Why do I have to take a pill which dulls my senses etc., but not actually correcting the underlining issue?

3. Why are these issues continuing to rise world-wide and more so in the U.S.?

And the list goes on...

If my job is done correctly with this tool, then even if it helps one person who reads this (in which it has many times over during the years) then it was worth its release in book form.

START

The Mind Configurator is very similar in operation to how a computer works at its minute level.

At the center of a computer you have the CPU, which is the Central Processing Unit. This would be equivalent to your brain in operation. Handling many tasks in which some you are aware of consciously and others are being run in the background as you go about your day without even noticing. Some of these background processes are digestion, saliva production and the list goes on.

These aforementioned tasks of a computer are called sub-routines in which the sub-routines of your brain would be your subconscious. Through adept level meditation one learns how to observe the inner workings of these sub-routines at worst and at best are able to directly affect the on-goings of the sub-conscious mind for better or worse.

Via The Mind Configurator this will allow the beginner as well as the adept to call upon the sub-routines, the subconscious mind to understand thought processes to change behaviors and much more.

This book will focus on the sub-routine of thee emotional state.

The main avenues for simplicity sake will be positive, negative and neural.

Even though I have put rather detailed figures in the coming pages it would still be a good idea for you to write each out yourself as you follow along (extra blank pages in back of book for this purpose).

I also encourage you to write within the pages of this book as you would your own notebook.

Fig. 01

Emotions

This will be are start, please write this at top of a blank page.

LEVEL 1

Fig. 02

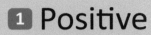

Fig. 03

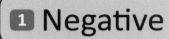

Fig. 04

LEVEL 2

In Level 2 we begin to branch outward into the second level of The Min Configurator.

When one makes The Mind Configurator it should be as precise an focused on the end result as possible. The more detailed you're in fig uring out what the next level may be the greater recall and change wi occur when The Mind Configurator is complete.

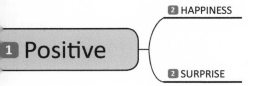

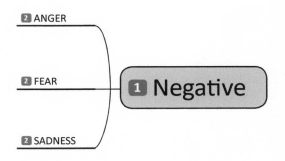

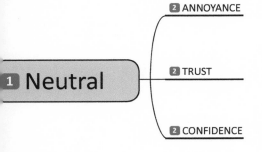

LEVEL 3

As we now venture into the 3rd level we dig deeper for more defining sub-routines. To further enable exploration of our mind.

Fig. 08

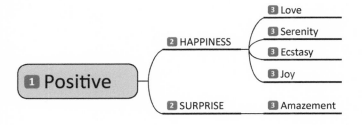

Fig. 09

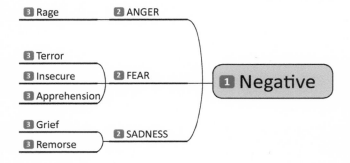

Fig. 10

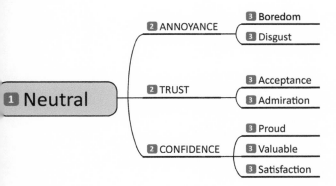

LEVEL 4

You will notice that in this level not all of the main attributes (i.e. Positive, Negative, Neutral) have a 4th level. And that is okay. Sometimes you may exhaust any further reach into certain aspects of your configurator. What I suggest is when this occurs step away for a period of time or even come back the next day with a fresh mindset to verify that indeed it is no further you can proceed.

Fig. 11

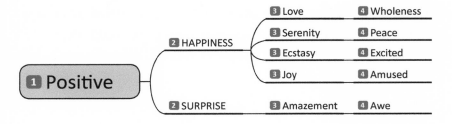

Fig. 12

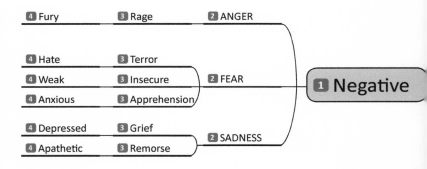

LEVEL 5

Level 5 will be the last level to the books configurator. As mentioned previously some configurators go more than a dozen levels deep. Less or more is not the sign of a configurator that has been created incorrectly and not every configurator can be applied to everyone as minds have slight differences.

Fig. 13

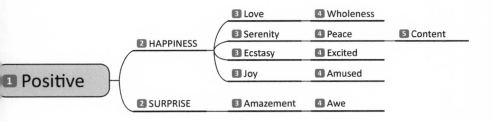

Fig. 14

NAMING

After the completion of The Mind Configurator via normal means as shown previously, the most important part is naming the sub-routines of your configurator.

The naming in an easily re-memorable and with personal significance will increase the potential of your configurator as a tool. A configurator that was haphazardly created would be as a automobile with flat tires. Yes it is a automobile and yes it has tires but it won't take you far. There is no rush.

You would want to name the sub-routines with something that you can't run out of. As an example naming them with shapes you may find difficulty after rather quickly to come up with new shapes so you will either have to start your naming process over or change it to something else half way through which shows no uniformity and leads to a less powerful configurator.

Names or numbers are best to use with the majority of configurators. And between names and numbers, names are better to use because they can be personal and the more personal the better.

For the examples to follow we will be naming our sub-routines with the names of Angels and Demons from the Christian religion.

Why?

Because most of the western world is familiar with Christianity so many will find it memorable in one way or another.

Fig. 15

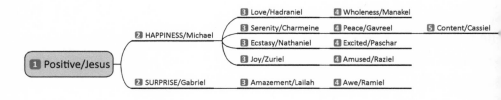

Fig. 16

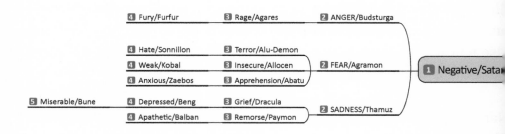

Fig. 17

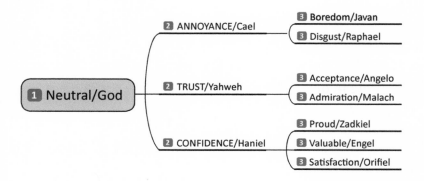

As you see in figure 15-17 there are biblical names (Christianity based) next to sub-routines above.

So the main sub-routine attribute of positivity is 'Jesus' which when called upon is bringing about activity from all the sub-routines that it governs. But to enact the change that is needed we need to go a bit deeper. There is nothing wrong with calling on the name of the main attribute for discovery, but ideally you would want to narrow down the specific sub-routine for the answer or action that you want to pursue.

So as an example; you met someone that you just fell head over heels in love with which is great. But you want to know why do you feel this way. So the love sub-routine above has the name of 'Hadraniel'.

Some questions to ask Hadraniel who governs the sub-routine of love are:

1. Hadraniel, is this actually love that you feel?
2. Hadraniel, if it is indeed love, why do you feel this way?

In accessing your sub-consciousness in this manner, it has no choice but to give you an answer. This answer may come in the form of a direct communication from your subconscious mind and/or a dream and/or conscious thought throughout your day.

But let's make this bit more complex. Let's say that Hadraniel who governs love and is all love, and nothing more or less is feeling insecure so in-turn, you're insecure. Well the insecurity sub-routine is governed by 'Allocen'. So the next step would be to ask Allocen (insecurity) who is a sub-routine of Satan (Negativity) the following:

1. Allocen, why are you feeling insecure about Hadraniel?
2. Allocen, did Hadraniel do something to you?
3. Allocen, what can we do to bring you to peace?

Now to add yet another scenario into this drama is that as you were asking Hadraniel (love) about the insecurity (Allocen) felt because you were just so head over heels for someone because you felt this is your soul mate without any doubt in the world, acceptance and trust came over you. Angelo (Acceptance) and Yahweh (Trust) which are sub-routines put all at ease.

As you took a look at your configurator you took note that these two are sub-routines of the God (Neutral). And as such by their very nature of being neutral and overseeing this internal dialogue (drama) that was playing out interjected to bring Acceptance and Trust.

Which in the end, you now understand there's no need for Agramon (Fear) to be anywhere near the way you're feeling.

Hundreds more of simple to complex examples could be given and then even more could be thought of. In the end you will have to create a personal configurator for yourself to experience the internal changes that happen within when one finally is not living by why, what, when, where and how but in-fact living in the know of how their mind works from the subconscious level.

Not all configurators have to be personal, but for those that deal with emotional/mental/intellectual states of mind these should be as personal as possible. An example of this would be using the name of your mother and father, grandmother and grandfather and so forth. As such in this example when you call on these sub-routines you will be actually calling the members of your family which in-deed may bring about a more powerful transformation then any of the examples above.

This subconscious dialogue can be made more direct and take less time between answers via meditation/prayer on a regular basis. The more you're able to meditate/pray without external stimuli such as words or music being played in the background the more ease will be found in sub-conscious to conscious mind communication and the answers that spring forth.

CONCLUSION

As with many of my previous titles I purposely try to be as direct as possible without giving any fluff in reading material. As such this leads to books that are less in pages but every page being as important as the next.

I hope you found this to be true while reading The Mind Configurator.

As mentioned previously there are many other configurators such as mental and intellectual which are states of mentality. But other configurators exist such as those that deal with the physical body and even more that deal with life.

These more advanced configurators are typically cultivated during private events or consultations in which most if not all the participants are well versed in the workings of this tool and positive change has occurred numerous times within their life and that of their loved ones and patients.

Wishing you well.